CW01082640

Deanna Rodger is a leading poe
reimagined version of 'If' was rea
been welcomed to perform and
the world including Mexico, Suc
commissioned by institutions su
Young Vic, and BBC. She is a for.
and represented the UK for poetry at the International Biennale,
Rome 2011. She designs and delivers educational programs,
and tutors at the School of Communication Arts and is a
founding member of Keats House Poetry Forum and Chill Pill.
I Did It Too, a collection of performance poetry celebrating a
decade of work, came out in 2017 (Burning Eye Books). Theatre
commissions include *Now We Are Here* (Young Vic Dir. Ian
Rickson), and *Sing Before You Speak Again* (Young Vic).

Her Arts Council funded program Poetry Facilitation Training
is in development with an accompanying exploration of Why
Poetry Facilitation is important.

Follow her on social media @deannarodger for more information.

his fingers have left

Deanna Rodger

Burning Eye

BurningEyeBooks
Never Knowingly
Mainstream

This edition published by Burning Eye Books 2021

www.burningeye.co.uk
@burningeyebooks

Burning Eye Books

15 West Hill, Portishead, BS20 6LG

ISBN 978-1-913958-12-1

Book cover designed by Joanna Layla

For Kevin Elyot, whose creative past and process live on and on and on.

For my daughters.

Contents

INTRODUCTION

In May of 2018 I was eight months pregnant and overdue to move to Bristol from London. I was nervous for London to become a memory. I was uncertain of what this new time meant for me: my career, my friendships, my identity. A friend and colleague, knowing this, sent through a link to the Kevin Elyot residency at the University of Bristol Theatre Collection: £3,000 to explore an idea through Kevin Elyot's archive.

I spent a long of time digging into Elyot's work before applying. I was hyper-aware of our differences – white/black, male/female, gay/straight, Birmingham/London, old (deceased)/younger (alive) – and it was in these differences that I found our common ground.

After much deliberation (and backing from my mother-in-law), I applied. I figured I would need some income, I would need to get to know people and institutions in this new city, and I would want to explore and develop my writing.

I launched at poetry exploding with opinions. They directed my writing and performance. They are defiant opinions. They would squeeze into percussive rhyme schemes and confront audiences in live spaces. I knew how to perform these opinions. In the transformation from independence to mother, international jetsetter to Bristol stroller, fuck the world to save the world, I felt a pull to the quiet meditative space the page offers the reader and writer, and the reach a book can have if not tethered to a sleep-deprived mortal.

My aim was 'to study my own creative and reflective processes as they are reflected through another's, Elyot's'. This residency led me to interrogate my process in three ways: it 1) sparked an internal debate between idea and form, 2) challenged me to engage with poetry on the page in a way which was once haphazard and puzzled, and 3) pushed me to determine how important the distribution of ideas and information is to me as a creative. *his fingers have left* is a result of that exploration.

It is now 2021 as I write this introduction, I am a mother to two small children amid a pandemic. A time of rampant fear and mistrust, of loss and, delicately, of hope.

Not a gay playwright but a playwright who happened to be gay.

Kevin Elyot is a playwright who committed himself to his writing and the arts and wanted to contribute to someone else's passion. Born in Birmingham in 1951, in 1970 he moved to Bristol to read theatre studies at the University of Bristol. The University of Bristol was the first institution to offer a degree in theatre studies. It is home to one of the largest theatre history and live art archives in the world, of which Elyot's work is now a part.

The time in which art is created is often reflected in the nature of the piece, and Elyot's writing came out of a unique and long overdue moment in history. A moment of liberation for a body of marginalised people. A time of celebration of homosexual love and connection. A time when people and writing could go public, and when Elyot's writing did.

Elyot staged domestic dramas in which the central characters were gay. Not 'coming out' stories, but the story beyond. The lives of people compromised in the all-too-human tug between desire and love.

Elyot is renowned for his attention to structure, and his witty, frank and dark-humoured dialogue.

Incredibly private man. There is very little publicly known about his personal life.

Elyot died in 2014. The residency is centred around his extensive archive. I read the contents of this archive and was immediately struck by how thorough it seemed. It made me consider my legacy. What I will choose to leave behind, and why? Will I make it clear what is what, or will I choose to leave some thoughts ambiguous? Will I get a choice?

In the archive, I could find extraordinarily little of Elyot's personal life – the life outside theatre – and I found it frustrating not to be able to speak with the man himself. To ask him the blunt and difficult questions; to pry with certainty.

I have used the internet as much as if not more than his archive in order to find out about him. I suspect he was writing from real-life experience, as no matter how much we change – names, places, ages – we cannot help but write ourselves into everything we touch.

I wanted to get personal takes on this writer. Fortunately, I happened to know of someone who had worked with Elyot on a few of his plays.

his fingers have left is written in two sections.

Section 1 is a blend of poetry and a conversation between me and Ian Rickson, notable director and friend. There are five poems, written in direct response to five of Elyot's plays. As well as drawing inspiration from the plays themselves, I set myself rules in honour of the emphasis Elyot placed on style and form:

- Must be written from the perspective of an inanimate object.
- Must be written in a defined poetic form, though I have not always followed the traditional line breaks.
- Must be on the theme of sex.

Section 2 is a look into the making of these poems. Here you will find the story of each poem and how they were made. This section is my contribution to someone else's passion for writing. A kind of in-book residency!

The process of writing these poems was originally captured in my own special way on Instagram: @whoknowspoetry

This work was inspired and developed through the generous support of the Kevin Elyot award. This book is a token of appreciation to the team at Bristol Theatre Collection. I am so grateful to have been able to first interrogate and then expand my practice.

Thank you, reader. I hope this inspires you to create your own works.

SECTION 1

It was a play about nostalgia, love lost, about being haunted by past pleasures, and how, perversely, realising one's desires can doom you to a life living in the shadow of past fulfilments …

Simon Farquhar

Ian Rickson was artistic director at the Royal Court from 1998 to 2006. During this time Kevin Elyot staged Forty Winks, which was directed by Katie Mitchell.

Elyot and Ian had worked together previously at the National Theatre after being put together as playwright and director. Here they put on The Day I Stood Still. They also worked together on Mouth to Mouth.

I was interested in how the relationship between Ian and Elyot developed over time. I was also interested in learning more about how to approach venues: whether an idea should be fully formed or raw.

As luck would have it, Ian would be in Bristol, and so I invited him round for lunch to catch up, meet my then-baby and have a chat about Elyot. I recorded our conversation on my phone but knew that half of the content would remain private.

I reflected on this conversation often throughout the course of my residency. My idea of writing with the apparent personal came from this conversation.

Elyot's intention was clear; my work is the show.

IAN   I feel like 'how has been your day'.[1]

D   I was just thinking that.
        I have put the phone face down.
        There is something about not being able to see
        any of the light of it;

        after a while you just sink into
        just chatting.

        He kept meticulous notes on everything.

IAN   He was very thorough in that way.

D   …and that is what attracted me to him.

        There is not much crossover regarding his plays and
           my writing.
        It was him keeping all these meticulous notes that
           attracted me to the collection.
        I am thinking about process,

        trying to unpick my own process.

        I've got to the point where I need to look at what I am
           doing
        with a lens that can pull it apart and put it back
           together
        and teach it and be more conscious of it.

        All of his notebooks and all the reviews and all the
           cards,
        it's fascinating and bizarre,
        really personal, but

---

[1]   This was the first title for the play I wrote, directed by Ian, which ended up being called *Now We Are Here* (Young Vic, 2016).

IAN   I've got quite a clear sense of him.
I think I've directed two
and I saw the first one
which I was also offered.

He was a really tender, thoughtful—
he sort of wrote into [his] wound,
so then the first big success My Night With Reg was
about that
pre-wounded moment or sort of
special connection, then
something sullies or
destroys or

Birmingham. Bubbles. Street. Pop. Swell. Night

after Coming Clean

I found myself in Birmingham
in a case of bubbles.
Trolleyed along Broad Street,
my glass bottle ready to pop,
my cork squeezed desperate to swell.
It is Saturday night.
The Broad Street clubbers' night.
The eighteen-pluses of Birmingham
fill the queue, already pissed to swell,
bellies empty like bubbles,
wrapped tight in dresses whose colours pop.
I hear sharp heels on the street.
    'Moët, that's up my street!'
    'Let's make this our night and buy something we can pop.'
    'So you go to Birmingham University, the red brick bubble?'
    'This student loan has made my pocket swell.'
Cork popped to swell; somewhere a woman wees in the street.
Clink of cheers spills my bubbles. Settled on the lip of the night,
pulled to the throat of Birmingham, crunched by tongues till
    groins pop.
Drinkers beyond their means, they pop! And celebrate,
a third cork swell glugged into a taxi across Birmingham to
    drop her down her street.
Too wasted to close the night, she must ask him up, blow air in
    his bubbles.

A drunk fuck for his bubbles. Jeans unzip and dresses pop. Slip
latex over the night. Top her up with your swell. A harboured
silence falling over the street;

she's asleep
and won't be screwed awake. She's asleep; pull out and sleep as
    well.

Yank the wrapper off, head down. No! Leave. Spew into the
    street. Night, night.
She's asleep,
just,
        and the bubble pops in Birmingham.

IAN   My favourite is *The Day I Stood Still*.

It's very simple. It's got two time schemes,
the idea of
are you trapped in a memory
or can you live your life fully, particularly as a gay man?

Then I did another one, Mouth to Mouth,
although did it when I had babies,
so that was quite a difficult time,

but that's full of feeling too.

I like this thing he writes with a type of tight
economical style, but there's a lot of feeling underneath it.
Sort of Chekhov, I guess, would be his big influence.

THREE SUMMERS

after Twilight Song

She listens as the light fades:
the distant promise of a dream,
a bloodstain,
a gentle rustling of the tree.
The distant promise of a dream,
the penalty for a wasted life,
a gentle rustling of the tree.
Everything comes at a price.
The penalty for a wasted life –
the kind old sun nearly gone.
Everything comes at a price.
There's other worlds out there,
    worlds of wonder, but 'this is our lot,
the kind old sun nearly gone.
    A bloodstain.

There's other worlds out there, worlds of wonder,'
but this is our lot.
    She listens as the light fades.

IAN   He was really involved in all the plays.

       Then we put another one on called *Forty Winks*.
       It's 'A Case of You', isn't it?
       They keep listening to that song by Joni Mitchell.

       That idea of yearning for a moment of technicolour,
           fullness.

       There's a lot of longing and that kind of intense feeling
           about past.

       Plus he did write some really good tellies.
       One called *Clapham Junction* about being gay in Clapham
       and that kind of diaspora.

       I think he was really quite keen not to be pigeonholed as
       being a gay 'right-on' politically correct writer.
       He really wanted just his own creative autonomy.

VAUXHALL CORSA DRIVING OVER DARTFORD BRIDGE

after Forty Winks

I'm sorry my music won't play,
sorry that the Halfords man couldn't fix me,
sorry you've run out of things to say…
hope the grind of my engine sounds OK?
Put your foot on my clutch, move me up to gear three.

I'm sorry my music won't play.
Left hand gripping so tight like my body might sway.
Right one wipes and wipes so your feelings aren't seen.
Sorry.

You've run out of things to say
to the guy who can't drive, whose heart you can't save,
strapped in by your side in my passenger seat. 'I'm sorry my
music won't play. It's an ongoing problem; it's not just today.
You know in your view that it's not meant to be.
Sorry.'

You've run out of things to say sorry.
Driving doesn't make you brave,
doesn't sputter if you cheat.
I'm sorry my music won't play.
Sorry. You've run out of things to say.

IAN   I miss him.
        He was his own very caring, thoughtful, funny person.

        The National were doing that play, The Day I Stood Still.
        I enjoyed being very attentive to him as a kind of primary
            artist.
        He was in rehearsals a lot.
        He was fastidious.

        Tenacious.
        Maybe the way he wrote was the accruing of all these
            notes.
        Kevin was maybe more meticulous and planned and
            thought about it and then wrote,
        trying lots of ways to get the creative spirit to be borne.

        I got the completed script.

HIS FINGERS HAVE LEFT

after And Then There Were None

10

Revise this version of events. Your girl went
home and, pissed on Palais cocktails, you stayed out.
Bumped into a past link who happened to
be fiending for a pussy dine;
despite rumours of a shit bag you couldn't feel one
fucking into Christmas Day. He choked
you on his
dick whilst his tongue drunk-dialled your clit, and his little
finger now roams recklessly by itself.
Fifteen when you two went out, two-timed, dumped, and
you got checked at the clinic then.
You will need to return there.
Now face back to where you were
counting down to buss: 'Ten, nine...'

Your princess Disney diary gives me the evils sat
on the chest of drawers, teaching some sort of growing up.
Its code of 'p's for period and scribbled hands for fingering is very
thorough. You ain't had unprotected sex, but panic when late.
Look at me through the clumped mascara in your eye, and now the other one.
Tell that bully Mr Busby you're sorry, an accident, you overslept.
Remind him of the 'lock and throw away' version of himself,
of being human, and inexplicable and… and… unreliable, and
when he tuts at the bold mess of you holding out a pink punctuality slip then
take it and meet your girl in the locker rooms beneath the headmistress's office, and there
you'll slick baby hair down like enforced curfews cos you were
smartarsed enough to skip registration for clinic when it opened at eight.

First professional poetry trip. Fully paid for solo travelling,
lugging around a case of books to fit first-year uni revision in.
Lanyard of keys round your neck like the one stolen by Devon
summers ago when running was less heartbreak and Facebook. One
day you'll jump on an 87 bus and not miss his stop, your girl has said.
The boy chased you with your own lanyard of keys, and he'd
never promised to be the one to stay
there

alone. So you've gone to compete in a poetry slam in France and
found distance in a bunkbed. You figure you'll move on then.
Their son is almost one and your summer's been locked up. There
were call-abroad charges. Weighing the exchange rate, we're
too broke, and it's too late to place +44 in front of seven.

There is a fine art to chopping
red onions without welling up.
Google it. The bulb releases an irritant which sticks
to the tear duct, causing one
wannabe chef to weep. However, if chopped
with a sharp knife – by which I mean axed and left to himself –
or held clingfilmed captive in
a fridge until the pain is split to halves –
by which I mean fry the pale and
basic bitch with the caramel hair – then
add rice and garlic and kidney beans, simmer, and there
will come a time to serve, as it were,
at least to remove the pan from gas mark six.

6

Notes: She was only playing
homeless until she was with
child, and if psychic harm is a
physical threat then I am capitalism to a hive,
not that I had any idea I was a
doubting Thomas to her bumblebee
nest. She was my girl and I was stung
to not be the first one
told of this angel, to learn through an 'oh, and'
add-on, where you are chatting the scripture and then
the news is dropkicked as if there
is sin on your lips, or as if you were
an allergy that'd displace a foetus with a high-five.

I swear to tell a truth. She was going,
then he pulled up pissed on a 'ped and let her in.
I'll confess, she accused: *What are you drink-driving for?*
Asides from your dead mate, you're breaking the law.
On her life, she was courting the one.
She: nineteen, terminally lonely. He: twenty-five, got
his story dressed up after going in.
His record is for all to view in Chancery.
A well-cut trench coat and
fresh kicks, but when he sipped a rave of brandy then
he'd lash out. Well, that night he smashed my screen so sharp there
were scarlet voicemails all over the floor. Were
it not for her elastic sense of judgement, justice would've been forged by RJ at sixty-four.

Did you just check my time as he was going
down on you? You should kick him out.
That straightened hairdo will throw you into
rocky waters. Your love for this man is a sea
monster, as fictional as a
man bearing a sack of gifts wearing a red
suit. Whose ears will hear this herring
call? Fallen, pushed or swallowed:
regardless, you're the only one
who went along to play a part to plot and
who's schemed to depths that'll come out in the wash. Then
what? What shanty will you sing his son's mum twelve days from now: *There*
we were

on Christmas Eve. Unplanned. He dropped me home at three.

I had no idea how quick walking
was going to get you out of the relationship you were in,
leading you to home to grab the
spare key, mind a flaming zoo,
a feeling caught, a stampede as a
left foot slipped in front of a right, big
steps from a bullied girlfriend who will no longer bear
the weight spit and ash and fear hugged
around her chest. Asthmatic love like safety was one
stop too far, keep walking left, right and
breathe, a plan, a mission of stealth; go in and then
ascend and then look at his heaving body there,
sweating in his sickness as if he were
weeping for two.

2

You clutch me on silent, sitting
opposite Her mate. Her mate next to Her in
this quiet bar on Northcote Road. The
suggestion you should perform has me like the sun
too close to fair skin. One
moment we're 'the sideline ho' and the next we've got
centre stage – your frizzled
pulse betraying this one-up
uni-poem of love and
ambition, and it wasn't about him then,
but now it sounds like there
is a chaser heart, which there was
not. Round for round, Hers is the one
his fingers have left
to smash my inbox for an all-
egiance. A figural one.
An exodus he
abandoned. He went
pale-palmed to Her blackout,

an unassailable command

demoting your seraph's chorus which had hung

over the cherub himself

as a holy holiday shot for taken land.

I am the fallen burner, I am the heathen,

I am the Christmas plague, and I am the re-

velation of the covet. We re-

ceive and send texts from the finger of Her: *Why the fuck has he got ur phone?*

IAN   He waited.
       He really liked to do it himself,
       allowing each idea to crystallise in its form.

       He thrummed a level of tension,
       wanting it to be right.

AS THE POLISH MET THE RING

after The Perfect Moment

I liked the wait
for Derek, though
I'm purely practical.

I worry seriously
about 'perfect' –
is it going to be enough?

I mean, Derek's perfect,
but I'm bothered
about starting it,

fading down and coming
back – the end. I think
Derek's perfect.

Speaking over
the disappearance,
I thought more

than he said
and would later
want to know.

But I realise
that, as the polish
met the ring,

if there's a possible
alt – 'the one',
I would leave,

gladly, again.

SECTION 2
THE MAKING OF

BIRMINGHAM. BUBBLES. STREET. POP. SWELL. NIGHT

a sestina
after Coming Clean

This sestina is written from the perspective of a bottle of Moët.

Moved by William's horrific experience in Coming Clean, I chose to write about an occurrence that happened while I was in university in Birmingham, which had enlightened me with regard to the darker side of alcohol and consent when on a date. It was for this reason that I chose the form of a sestina.

What is a sestina?

This is a poem of six stanzas, each of six lines, with a three-line envoi at the end of the piece. The envoi in poetry is the moral or conclusion of the poem, summing up what the poem wants to get across.

The six words at the end of the lines of the first stanza will be repeated in different orders over the remaining stanzas. All the words are to be used in the three-line envoi. There are two different ways of writing the envoi, which I will show below. But remember to read some sestinas. You will notice that many people break the rules.

I think sestinas are beautiful and hypnotic, and, much like the effects of alcohol, the tight repetition of a few select words forces those words to become more of themselves in the space of a line. Often my initial relationship to each of the words is changed by the end of the poem.

How I wrote one

I got out a big workbook (A3 plain) and my trusted Sharpies. At the top of the page I wrote my concept and words associated with it. I drew thirty-nine lines (six blocks of six and one block of three) to scaffold the poem. At the end of each of these lines, I marked the order that the words would have to go in.

I then picked six words that I figured were key to the story I was going to write a sestina on. For my first draft these were *Birmingham*, *champ*, *street*, *pop*, *swell* and *night*. It was only after reading though and not being fully satisfied with how some of the sentences sounded that I decided to change champ to another term for champagne, *bubbles*.

The order for the end-of-line words in a sestina is this:

1st stanza: A B C D E F
2nd stanza: F A E B D C
3rd stanza: C F D A B E
4th stanza: E C B F A D
5th stanza: D E A C F B
6th stanza: B D F E C A
Envoi: there are many different interpretations as to how the words should be placed in this. What did my envoi pattern end up being?

she's asleep
and won't be screwed awake. She's asleep; pull out and sleep as well.
Yank the wrapper off, head down. No! Leave. Spew into the street. Night, night.
She's asleep,
just,
and the bubble pops in Birmingham.

Once the piece was written in rough on the paper, I typed it up and began to experiment with form to reflect content. What effect do you think this had on my poem?

Top tip for writing a sestina: think about what you want to write and then choose six words which you feel would lend themselves to numerous interpretations. Remember that these can change, but try to stick at them until you get a first draft.

THREE SUMMERS

a pantoum
after Twilight Song

This pantoum is from the perspective of a living-room sofa. In order to write this pantoum I used lines of dialogue found in the play itself.

A pantoum has a cyclical nature to it, like a villanelle, which we'll look at later, but in a pantoum the first line serves as the last line. This is like the nature of time inherent in *Twilight Song*. Its ABAB rhyme scheme runs through each quatrain and reminds me of the house Elyot made for some of the characters to double up.

What is a pantoum?

This form consists of four four-line stanzas which traditionally have a rhyme scheme of ABAB, although 'Three summers' doesn't rhyme.

There are eight different lines in total, which are repeated in a specific order:

1, 2, 3, 4
2, 5, 4, 6
5, 7, 6, 8
7, 3, 8, 1

The repetition of a pantoum is haunting and slow, and it revisits previous lines in the same way *Twilight Song* echoed within itself with themes of unfixable losses: of love and lust, friendship and youth, and parent and child.

How I wrote one

For my pantoum I took eight lines from Elyot's play *Twilight Song*. You can do this too! Or make up your own.

Write each line out twice on separate pieces of paper, as each line appears twice. Play with the order, working out where each line goes. It will also help if you draw a template, with the line pairs marked, to move the pieces of paper around on.

Top tip for writing a pantoum: think carefully about the first line, as it will also be the last line of the poem. How do you want the audience to have changed by that point?

VAUXHALL CORSA DRIVING OVER DARTFORD BRIDGE

a villanelle
after Forty Winks

This villanelle is written from the perspective of my (now scrapped) Vauxhall Corsa.

The villanelle form is repetitive and, echoing the themes in *Forty Winks*, there is a drag back to the first line, an inability to move forward. I wanted this piece to honour the mechanics of the vehicle and how it might feel being driven, how it feels that it does not measure up or is letting its driver down. No expert can fix this car.

What is a villanelle?

This is a nineteen-line poem, with four three-line stanzas and one final four-line stanza, though in my final edit for 'Vauxhall Corsa driving over Dartford Bridge' I chose to play with my line breaks.

The first and final lines of the first stanza are repeated in a pattern that I've laid out in the section below.

How I wrote one

Think of two lines that you wouldn't mind repeating. Label these A1 and A2. They will need to rhyme. Mine were:

A1: *I'm sorry my music won't play.*
A2: *Sorry you've run out of things to say.*

Draw a template and place the lines in the order given below. There will be gaps, marked by the empty *a* and *b* lines.

A1: *I'm sorry my music won't play*
b
A2: *Sorry you've run out of things to say*

a
b
A1: I'm sorry my music won't play

a
b
A2: Sorry you've run out of things to say

a
b
A1: I'm sorry my music won't play

a
b
A2: Sorry you've run out of things to say

a
b
A1: I'm sorry my music won't play
A2: Sorry you've run out of things to say

The game is to fill in the gaps whilst honouring the story and the rhyme scheme. All *a* lines should rhyme with each other (and with A1 and A2), and all *b* lines should rhyme with each other. You may have to change your starting lines.

Remember to read lots of other villanelles; you will notice that some rules get bent. Can you spot where I have bent a rule?

his fingers have left

a Golden Shovel
after And Then There Were None

This Golden Shovel is written from the perspective of a phone.

I chose this form to demonstrate what we take from other people. Terrance Hayes took Gwendolyn Brooks' poem and made the Golden Shovel. I have taken Hayes' idea and used the nursery rhyme Agatha Christie took to serve as the plot for her bestselling novel *And Then There Were None*. Kevin Elyot took Agatha Christie's novel to turn it into a play.

Those familiar with the nursery rhyme will notice that I have removed an adjective and a deeply offensive noun. I chose not to replace these.

The absence of something bad does not make good but clears space. We are always recreating, reimagining what has already been and borrowing from the world around us. I ask, how do we make better?

I used the style of the killings as written by Agatha Christie when writing each of the stanzas.

What is a Golden Shovel?

A Golden Shovel is a contemporary form of poem, created by Terrance Hayes when he took Gwendolyn Brooks' poem 'We Real Cool' and wrote a new piece of poetry in which the last word of each line, read in order, formed the original poem (twice over!). Kind of like a backwards acrostic poem which uses whole words rather than letters.

How I wrote one

You can take lines (or poems) from any source if you want to; I took an entire nursery rhyme! What is important is that you try to honour and give reference to the original piece it was taken from.

Don't forget to play with form and line breaks, as some words may contain the word that you need the line to end on! And check out *The Golden Shovel Anthology* (University of Arkansas Press, 2017), edited by Peter Kahn, Ravi Shankar and Patricia Smith, with a foreword from Terrance Hayes.

Top tip for writing a Golden Shovel: there are some great websites which automatically find words that start with, contain and end with other words. This was super useful for me as the nursery rhyme repeated a lot of words, and I wanted to surprise my reader and stay faithful to the narrative.

AS THE POLISH MET THE RING

an erasure poem
after The Perfect Moment

This erasure poem is written from the perspective of a letter Elyot received with regard to *The Perfect Moment*.

I imagine this letter may have been anticipated. As an artist I know that feeling well: the feeling of checking my emails for replies on projects, hoping that they will be made and will be the one to launch me into stability, but there is no such thing.

There is nothing online about *The Perfect Moment* as it was never made. Written in 1988, it would have been erased from history if Elyot had not saved his work and given it to the Theatre Collection. Creation is a process of 'starting it, fading down, and coming back'. Elyot's award-winning career is a testament to that.

What is an erasure poem?

An erasure poem is created by deleting words from an existing piece of text. These, and similar poems, are sometimes called 'found' poems. They are poems which are made from another's words.

I decided to write this poem as, in *The Perfect Moment*, Molly seems influenced by Muriel's conversation to break up with her fiancé, Derek, but we never see the break-up. It is not spoken about. Letters often serve better than conversations, giving people the space to reflect on what is being communicated.

How I wrote one

I asked Athene at the Theatre Collection to photocopy the letter five times. I then set to reading and rereading. I was nervous to erase anything until I remembered that I could always begin again.

I challenged myself not to use 'I'm sorry' or 'I am glad that you're happy' as I felt that these were not only obvious choices, given my subject matter, but restricted the poem I could extract from the letter.

Set yourself parameters and, if it is strikingly obvious, save that version and start again without using those lines.

Here is the original letter. What poem would you make from this letter?

Don't forget, you too can visit the Theatre Collection in Bristol and explore Kevin Elyot's archive!

BROADCASTING HOUSE
LONDON W1A 1AA
TELEPHONE 01 580 4468 TELEX
TELEGRAMS & CABLES
BROADCASTS LONDON TE

Kevin Elyot   11/02/88
32 Parliament Hill
London NW3 2TN

Dear Kevin Elyot   RADIO DRAM
                                                  BBC

I'm sorry not to have been in touch before but Caroline
passed on the script in December when I was very busy in
~~the studio, and then Christmas came - between it and me and~~
I'm only now getting on with reading scripts.

I like the play very much indeed and the dinner between
Muriel and Molly is just terrific. And the waiter is a
marvellous character and I even got to be fond of poor
Derek, though I'm relieved for both of them that they didn't
get wed.

There are only a few things that worry me, and one is purely
practical - the thought of the expense of the Ferranti
Brothers! But I worry more seriously about both the perfect
moments - is a minute of the Bach going to be enough or will
it actually be too long? That sounds daft but I hope you
understand what I mean. And Derek's perfect moment - with
the advent of C.D's we can use a recording, though it may
not be possible to have the John Ireland but I'm bothered
about the idea of starting it, fading down and then coming
back for the end, which I think will sound pretty naff.
But would Derek spoil his perfect mement by speaking over
the choir?

Muriel's disappearance: I thought perhaps Dennis knew more
than he said and would later reveal where she'd gone and
I wanted to know. But I realise that it's better that she
just goes, as the Polish seaman did. That's a query only,
but perhaps you could think about it too.

We met in the George didn't we - with Tom Wilkinson? It
would be very good to meet again, but February and March
are fairly crowded months for me. Do you think you could
give me a ring and see if there's a possible day because
although the play won't be done until the summer I wouldn't
want to leave it that long.

Thanks very much for the play and I'm glad that you're
happy for me to direct it.

Yours sincerely

p.p Jane Morgan

BROADCASTING HOUSE
LONDON W1A 1AA
TELEPHONE: 01 580 4468 TELEX: 265781
TELEGRAMS & CABLES
BROADCASTS LONDON TELEX

Kevin Elyot
32 Parliament Hill
London NW3 2TN

11/02/88

RADIO DRAMA
BBC

Dear Kevin Elyot

I'm sorry not to have been in touch before but Caroline
passed on the script in December when I was very busy in
the studio, and then Christmas came - anyway, and me sad
I'm only now getting on with reading scripts.

I like the play very much indeed and the dinner between
Muriel and Molly is just terrific. And the waiter is a
marvellous character and I even got to perform of your
Derek, though I'm pleased for both of them that they didn't
get wed.

There are only a few things that we ... and one is purely
practical ... the thought of it ... the Derek
scene. And I worry more seriously about both the perfect
moment - is the advent of the CD going to be enough ... will
it actually be too long? That sounds daft but I hope you
understand what I mean. And Derek's perfect moment - with
the advent of C.D. we can use recording, though it may
not be possible to have the John Ireland but I'm bothered
about the idea of starting it, fading down and then coming
back for the end, which I think will sound pretty naff.
But would Derek spoil his perfect moment by speaking over
the song?

Muriel's disappearance: I thought perhaps Dennis knew more
than he said and would later reveal where she'd gone and
I wanted to know. But I realise that it's better that she
just goes, as the Polish seaman did. That's a query only,
but perhaps you could think about it too.

We met in the George didn't we, with Tom Wilkinson? It
would be very good to meet again, but February and March
are fairly crowded months for me. Do you think you could
give me a ring and see if there's a possible day because
although the play won't be done until the summer I would't
want to leave it that long.

Thanks very much for the play and I'm glad that you're
happy for me to direct it.

Yours sincerely

Jane Morgan

ACKNOWLEDGEMENTS

Dean Atta for sending me the details of the Kevin Elyot award. Always having an eye out for me and many others.

Ruth Merttens for letting me send you my application over and over and over!

Mon Merttens for your extraordinary support, shifting your work patterns to care for our family.

Joanna Layla for your texts on Sunday 25 November 2020 reminding me to show off, and what a fine cover to do so with!

Ian Rickson, you are so kind and generous with your time and experience. Thank you for breaking bread with me.

Bridget Hart at Burning Eye for diving into these poems and saying yes! Wow, I really am very lucky.

John Berkavitch for asking, 'What do you want this to do?' That chat made this what it now is.

Harriet Evans for going through this so thoroughly and definitely clarifying some of my wild explanations of form!

Jo Elsworth for the kindest welcome into the Theatre Collection and trust in my sometimes AWOL process.

Athene and Jill for the archive chats, nothing ever seeming a bother, and letting me in on Mondays!

Pauline Lee for the love you share for your brother.